Tony Bailie

Mountain Under Heaven

SurVision Books

First published in 2020 by
SurVision Books
Dublin, Ireland
Reggio di Calabria, Italy
www.survisionmagazine.com

Copyright © Tony Bailie, 2020

Cover image © Maurice Burns, 2020

Design © SurVision Books, 2020

ISBN: 978-1-912963-09-6

This book is in copyright. No part of this publication may be reproduced, stored in a retrieval system, or transmitted in any form or by any means without the prior permission in writing from the publisher.

Acknowledgements

Grateful acknowledgement is made to the editors of the following, in which some of these poems, or versions of them, originally appeared:

Blue Fifth Review, Boyne Berries, A New Ulster, The Seventh Quarry, and *SurVision*. The Sweeney King sequence is part of a 'digital poetry collaboration' incorporating words, music and images, and can be found on YouTube.

CONTENTS

Mountain Under Heaven	5
Night Sizzles	6
Scorched Skin	7
Bleeding Fool	8
Fractured Folklore	9
Binary Affair	10
Washed Up	11
Premonition	12
Duende	13
Helix	14
Sweeney King	15
Church Music	22
Shrine	23
Calle Bolaño	24
Scrolls	25
The Smuggler	26
Louve	27
Star Aleph 151169	28
Ash	30
Destination	31
Managua	32
Hungry Ghost	33

Mountain Under Heaven

For Sinead

As world-changing events
unfold on TV
I sit cross-legged
and cast the I Ching
hoping to establish a counterflow,
not with any sense of faith
or belief
but a stand against the rational
a bid to surf on chaos...

Hexagram 33 – Tun:
mountain under heaven,
the image of retreat,
and so
the superior man
keeps the inferior from him,
not with anger
but reserve.

Night Sizzles

Sodium glow swirling,
yellow-tinted spiral of light
that twists and slithers
like urine down a drain,
gurgles into darkness.
Night sizzles, undulating,
electric shimmer,
tangible like static.
My hair stands on end
and I'm nervy in this sullen heat
as if possessed
and about to leap
into the rays of a black sun.

Scorched Skin

Between the curve of wilted leaf
and last ray of the sun
a fracture in the evening opens
with a half-heard creak,
a shuffling in a copse of trees
a ripple through a field.

Startled cattle swish their tails
and moan low warnings,
nesting crows rise and craw
above their shrieking chicks,
flapping in crooked spirals,
maternal ties abandoned.

She bathes to wash her scorched skin,
a faint smell of burning
rising from the mountain stream.

She beckons to me.

Bleeding Fool

Wine and blue-veined cheese
on a tenth-floor balcony,
flesh-red sky,
the city is in flames.
Stale and languid,
the night dilates,
a room in Hotel El Greco
swaddled in black sheets.
The bleeding fool led
from crowded side streets
into the public square.
Execution by stoning.
Stone-cracked head,
a self-mocking grin
runs like a scar,
the wound of laughter.

Fractured Folklore

Four swans in a broken V,
hollow wingbeat,
early morning flight.

Stepmother fatwa,
a witch's curse upon them.

Cloaked in feathers,
shamans chanting dreamtime,
they rest upon a foreign shore
their story scattered
like breaking tide,
fractured folklore ebbing,
washed from memory.

Binary Affair

Her pupils are tiny pinpricks of black,
twin dark stars
from another universe
drawn into parallel orbit
around our sun,
impenetrable specks of diamond
from which no light escapes,
compact and dense,
their gravity pulling me in
to a place where time has warped
and space is squeezed,
where the din of city traffic
has been compressed into a solar wind
that carries me
on an interstellar roar,
flaying and helpless
I am flung through her inner space,
hurled out sobbing and bleeding.

Washed Up

Drying out, I flapped like a seal
washed up on a rocky shore,
ocean ebbing from me,
a tide of horror and pounding delirium roar.
Hardening salt encrusts my skin,
bleached carapace tightens
and I am squeezed of all moisture,
arid and helpless.

Premonition

Time lurks, a shadow
in a half-opened doorway
waiting to swoop and engulf
the raw, unrefined night,
when all is still potential,
the shape of events unmoulded,
mere suggestions
of memories to come.

Duende

She falls into chaos
plunges freely,
writhing and kicking,
arms flailing,
flamenco dancer semaphore,
a call to follow her.

Helix

City streets loop and spiral
a DNA helix
curling and weaving in and out of itself
identity fractured
the essential I-ness gathered up and hurled
into the fractal swirl
a mesh of directions
that tangle and merge
and drift into flaying strands of snake-hair
a bag woman on a rain-drenched hill
I pass
avoiding stone-turning eyes
faint odour of sweat and stale piss
the hiss of wind whipping her hair
slurp of chapped lips
on the butt of a fag
fallen Medusa in winter.

Sweeney King

I

He lies as cold as a fledgling in snow
cast from its nest to shiver and weep
abandoned and
stripped of all love,
reborn as Sweeney.

II

His skin has been gouged by bramble and briar,
torn by wind-whipped thorn,
plucked open by whin and frozen by snow,
flesh, raw and on fire.
Naked and bleeding and half alive
he shivers under a bush
blood drops quiver like new-sprung blooms
stolen bundles of fruit.

III

He sips from a pool
and watches his face glide,
concentric rings slip in waves,
his beaked face and outstretched wings
shimmer in broken water.

Stillness returns
and fragments gather.

He pecks to scatter the startled face of a man.

IV

The rooks chant vespers
in their leafy stalls,
black-cowled monks,
pagan prayers croaked to their crow-god Sweeney.
Late comers circle in twilight,
dark angels among elms
caw throaty hymns of praise.

V

Sweeney still and heron-like,
rigid on a river bank,
reflecting on the water.
Half-caged in a row of reeds,
the current tugging at his knees,
he stands in meditation.
A vision of another life,
a half-dream in the twilight,
the mad man sobs in his cell.

VI

Red-eyed Sweeny cackles
chewing on cud of blackberry and sloe,
muddied in the ditch he buries his head in browning bracken.
Scrawny legs twitch in the cold
as the monk-cursed king whistles words,
his scab-torn skin plucked and featherless again.
Flapping arms, earthbound, human and insane,
naked on the roadside.

VII

Trussed by rope and wire,
tattered wings splayed and bound,
Sweeney lies crucified.
His captors probe his open beak
and shine lights in his eyes,
pluck at his skin and twist his neck
and latch clips to his side.
Then comes the fire and frying flesh,
the searing of his brain -
he flails and fights against his ties
as lightning strikes again.
The captors leave and Sweeny writhes
and falls into a swoon
the birdman curls into a ball
choking in the smoke-filled room.

Church Music

one-eyed crow claws
a taut line of gut
from a writhing rat
a vibrating string
arpeggio agony
a hidden note in a requiem
funeral black mass
psychedelic eucharist
consecrated rot-gut wine
pagan nun cups
blood-stained candles -
i give my benediction

Shrine

Your hair is flayed
a chaos of curls,
a lone tendril
that scars a cheek,
eyes dazed
and gazing to some other place,
a slow grimace
and then a coming to
as you sigh the memory from you.
We part in the hotel car park
and I am left
recalling a night
of Indian food
and corked red wine,
fumbled buttons
and a crumpled shrine
of sheets and pillows
on which you splayed
like a sacrifice,
aloof from the scene
from which you had already fled.

Calle Bolaño

The life has been sucked out
of this narrow street
where only vagrant weeds
splay like drug-addled hookers and rent boys
fucked lifeless by shadows.
Here daylight is just a rumour
and even rats stay away
refusing to scuttle in dank doorways
where in the flicker of a streetlight
the hint of a figure shimmers,
hovering beside the abyss.

Scrolls

Crisp leaves rustle,
copper pendants
inscribed with a secret alphabet,
their muffled secrets whispered
as I kick
my way along the street.

Later I return,
rain-soaked
and shuffling,
on a sponge of mulch,
slipping on
drowned mysteries.

The Smuggler

His twisted torso bends as he hauls a sack
and struggles to cross a mountain pass,
the Devil's Punchbowl.
Creased brow folds,
a furrowed landscape etched onto his face
as the dogs close in.

Louve

Kohl'd eyes darken and rouge lips
contract into a grimace,
sullen pout and angry hiss
as she twists her face from me,
pulling strands of untamed hair
she mutters incantations
and sniffs the air,
a she-wolf emerging.
Her woven piebald cloak of hemp
slips from her human frame,
the louve snarls and turns upon
her cowering prey.

Star Aleph 151169

A draft from a dungeon
carries a lone voice,
whispered pleas for freedom
that mix and swirl
with a cloud of dust
captured in a shaft of light,
a universe summonsed
by the swish of a rat's tail.
Four inches from the floor
above a moulding sack
lies a galaxy
with 10 billion stars
in the shape of the symbol Om
and in a segment of space
called the Ox's Horn,
by those who can observe it,
orbiting a blazing sun
lies a mountainous world
with rivers and forests
and huge churning seas
where winged creatures
flit among the trees
and sharp-toothed beasts hunt
foragers that
nestle among fallen leaves.
Sitting in a musky wood
just below a mountain pass
in a hidden, shallow cave
where candles burn

and bells chime,
a cowled figure in a half trance
listens to the forest's groan,
the creaking bark,
a dusty cough,
a prisoner moaning in his cell.

Ash

Bruised knuckles bulge
on brittle branches,
festering knots
tensed and waiting
for their locks to be sprung,
to spew their store
of infant leaves,
sprawl and suckle
on April rain,
then stretch out in the sun
and shuffle in a breeze,
cast shifting shadows
that gather and devour
those who lurk beneath them.

Destination

Tendrils of weed
haul the rusted axle
down to earth,
encasement of clay,
the memory of daytrips
and blurred open roads
fractured and flaking,
clumps of nettle
and dandelion clusters
smother once glinting steel,
machine-wrought precision
mangled and blistered,
journey's end
in an overgrown field.

Managua

Throat-clogging dust swirls
in coned eddies,
mini-tornadoes that rise
and twirl in spiralled hoops
that suddenly collapse
and scatter chaos.
Acrid smoke
seers my eyes,
snakes in wisps,
drifting tendrils
wrap themselves around me,
lassoes cast
by spectral captors
who rise from the haze
of embers and smoke
to hover by a bonfire.

Hungry Ghost

Her powdered skin
left a musky streak
across my crumpled sheet
that I didn't clean for a week,
the faint whiff of her
lingering when I bent to sniff
before going to sleep,
the memory of our disastrous rut –
separate rhythms
that never merged
into a unified flow –
a hungry ghost hovering,
burnt-out memories
carried on a waft of ash,
that settled on my bed.

More poetry published by SurVision Books

Noelle Kocot. *Humanity*
(New Poetics: USA)
ISBN 978-1-9995903-0-7

Ciaran O'Driscoll. *The Speaking Trees*
(New Poetics: Ireland)
ISBN 978-1-9995903-1-4

Helen Ivory. *Maps of the Abandoned City*
(New Poetics: England)
ISBN 978-1-912963-04-1

Elin O'Hara Slavick. *Cameramouth*
(New Poetics: USA)
ISBN 978-1-9995903-4-5

John W. Sexton. *Inverted Night*
(New Poetics: Ireland)
ISBN 978-1-912963-05-8

Afric McGlinchey. *Invisible Insane*
(New Poetics: Ireland)
ISBN 978-1-9995903-3-8

George Kalamaras. *That Moment of Wept*
ISBN 978-1-9995903-7-6

Anton Yakovlev. *Chronos Dines Alone*
(Winner of James Tate Poetry Prize 2018)
ISBN 978-1-912963-01-0

Bob Lucky. *Conversation Starters in a Language No One Speaks*
(Winner of James Tate Poetry Prize 2018)
ISBN 978-1-912963-00-3

Christopher Prewitt. *Paradise Hammer*
(Winner of James Tate Poetry Prize 2018)
ISBN 978-1-9995903-9-0

Mikko Harvey & Jake Bauer. *Idaho Falls*
(Winner of James Tate Poetry Prize 2018)
ISBN 978-1-912963-02-7

Anatoly Kudryavitsky. *Stowaway*
(New Poetics: Ireland)
ISBN 978-1-9995903-2-1

Maria Grazia Calandrone. *Fossils*
Translated from Italian
(New Poetics: Italy)
ISBN 978-1-9995903-6-9

Sergey Biryukov. *Transformations*
Translated from Russian
(New Poetics: Russia)
ISBN 978-1-9995903-5-2

Alexander Korotko. *Irrazionalismo*
Translated from Russian
(New Poetics: Ukraine)
ISBN 978-1-912963-06-5

Anton G. Leitner. *Selected Poems 1981–2015*
Translated from German
ISBN 978-1-9995903-8-3

Tim Murphy. *The Cacti Do Not Move*
(New Poetics: Ireland)
ISBN 978-1-912963-07-2

Tony Kitt. *The Magic Phlute*
(New Poetics: Ireland)
ISBN 978-1-912963-08-9

All our books are available to order via
http://survisionmagazine.com/books.htm

www.ingramcontent.com/pod-product-compliance
Lightning Source LLC
Chambersburg PA
CBHW061313040426
42444CB00010B/2619